fencing with the moon

by

Julie Schwerin

Finishing Line Press
Georgetown, Kentucky

fencing with the moon

*Dedicated to the women in my life, fore and aft:
Florence, Gladys, Judy, Noelle, Sydney, Gina,
Rachel, Megan, Rachel, Beth, Eva …*

Copyright © 2025 by Julie Schwerin
ISBN 979-8-89990-289-5 First Edition
All rights reserved under International and Pan-American Copyright Conventions. No part of this book may be reproduced in any manner whatsoever without written permission from the publisher, except in the case of brief quotations embodied in critical articles and reviews.

ACKNOWLEDGMENTS

Grateful acknowledgment is made to the editors of the following journals and publications in which some of these poems appeared:

Acorn, Akitsu Quarterly, A Hundred Gourds, Bones, Bottle Rockets, Cattails, #FemkuMag, Hedgerow, Human/Kind, is/let, Lyrical Passion, Mariposa, Mayfly, Modern Haiku, Mu, Prune Juice, Sheila-na-gig Online, Tinywords, Trash Panda, tsuri-dōrō, Voice of the River Valley, and *Whiptail.*

ARTIST'S STATEMENT

The poems in *Fencing With the Moon* draw inspiration from Japanese short-form poetry, particularly haiku, often described as "one-breath poems." Haiku utilizes the juxtaposition of two distinct parts as a tool for comparison.

The accompanying suminagashi artwork is a creation of the poet. Suminagashi, (literally "floating ink"), is a Japanese marbling technique which uses India ink to paint on water. The artist's process involves placing ink on the water's surface with a brush and introducing an agent to disperse it. Various factors, such as the amount of dispersant, water temperature, air currents, dust particles, brush angle, and contact time, influence the ink's spread and the resulting image. Suminagashi is a meditative practice for the artist, where the need to control outcomes is released, allowing the ink to paint freely. This unconventional creative process lacks preconceived notions or a specific goal, with the artist discovering the generated results after the fact—a process that yields surprising gifts.

Publisher: Leah Huete de Maines
Editor: Christen Kincaid
Cover Art: Julie Schwerin
Author Photo: Dan Schwerin
Cover Design: Elizabeth Maines McCleavy

Order online: www.finishinglinepress.com
          also available on amazon.com

Author inquiries and mail orders:
Finishing Line Press
PO Box 1626
Georgetown, Kentucky 40324
USA

fencing with the moon

you all in white
me I wouldn't dare

half a century
this advancing—retreating

until at last your thrusts
no longer draw blood

and   we   disengage

me

now as close
as I will ever come
to being

a man

THE SUNFLOWER TURNS

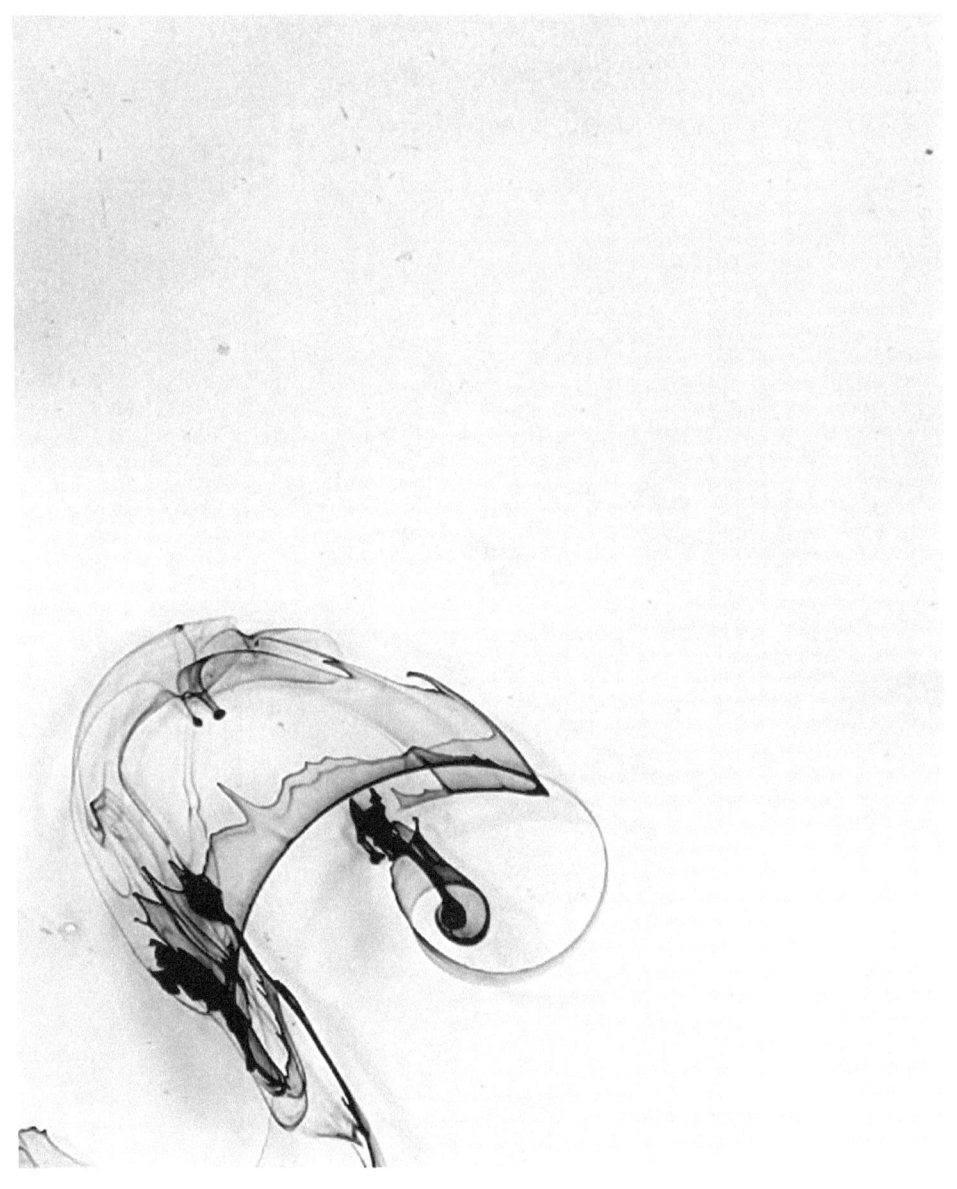

her tender years
the tremor of twilight
in a moonflower

long-stemmed red roses
she leaves the guard petals
intact

under the same sky he insists is red

birdsong editing my dream diary

the sunflower turns
how easily she accepts
his lie

her something blue
she chooses a gown
  with long sleeves

in her eyes
what doesn't show
on the x-ray

DANDELION WISHES

cockleburs ...
words he doesn't
remember saying

cheeseless maze—
believing this time
will be different

dandelion wishes
despite all my therapy
he's no better

end of summer
dumping the moon
back in the well

narrowing river
we learn to identify
his triggers

possessing a restraining order 9/10 of the law

susan's black eyes all that's left of September

THE INSIDE OF A TULIP

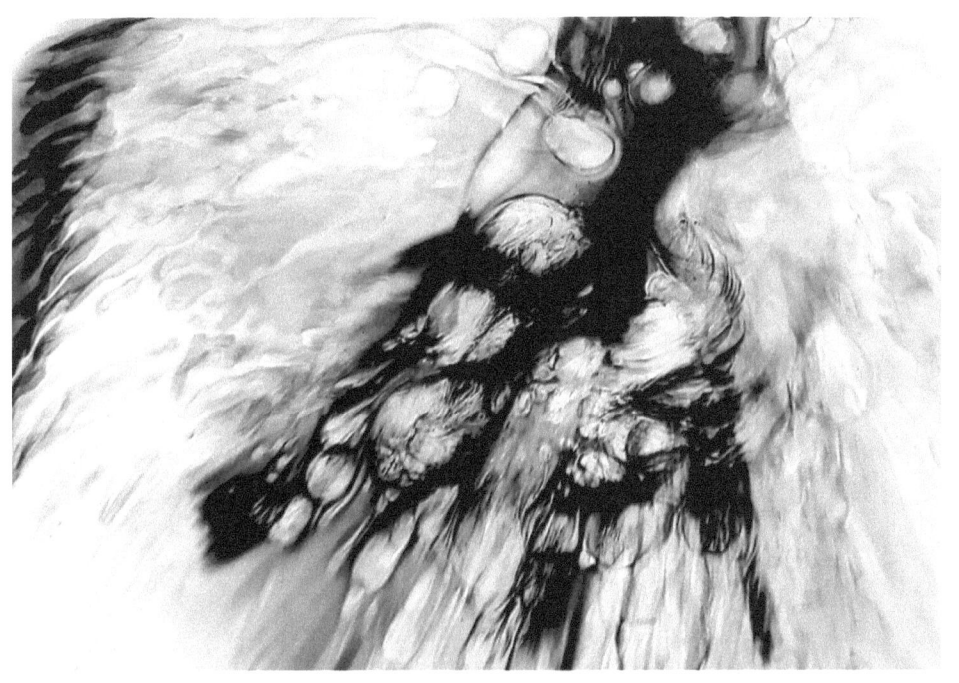

all day rain
his adjectives slip into
my vocabulary

storm clouds the inside of a tulip

untouched wilderness
being alone
with him

end of the daylily curling up with my loneliness

painted clouds …
the pause before
answering "fine"

endless sky
the hawk's gaze
on its tether

day moon
the only witness
remains silent

A HOLE IN THE LIGHT

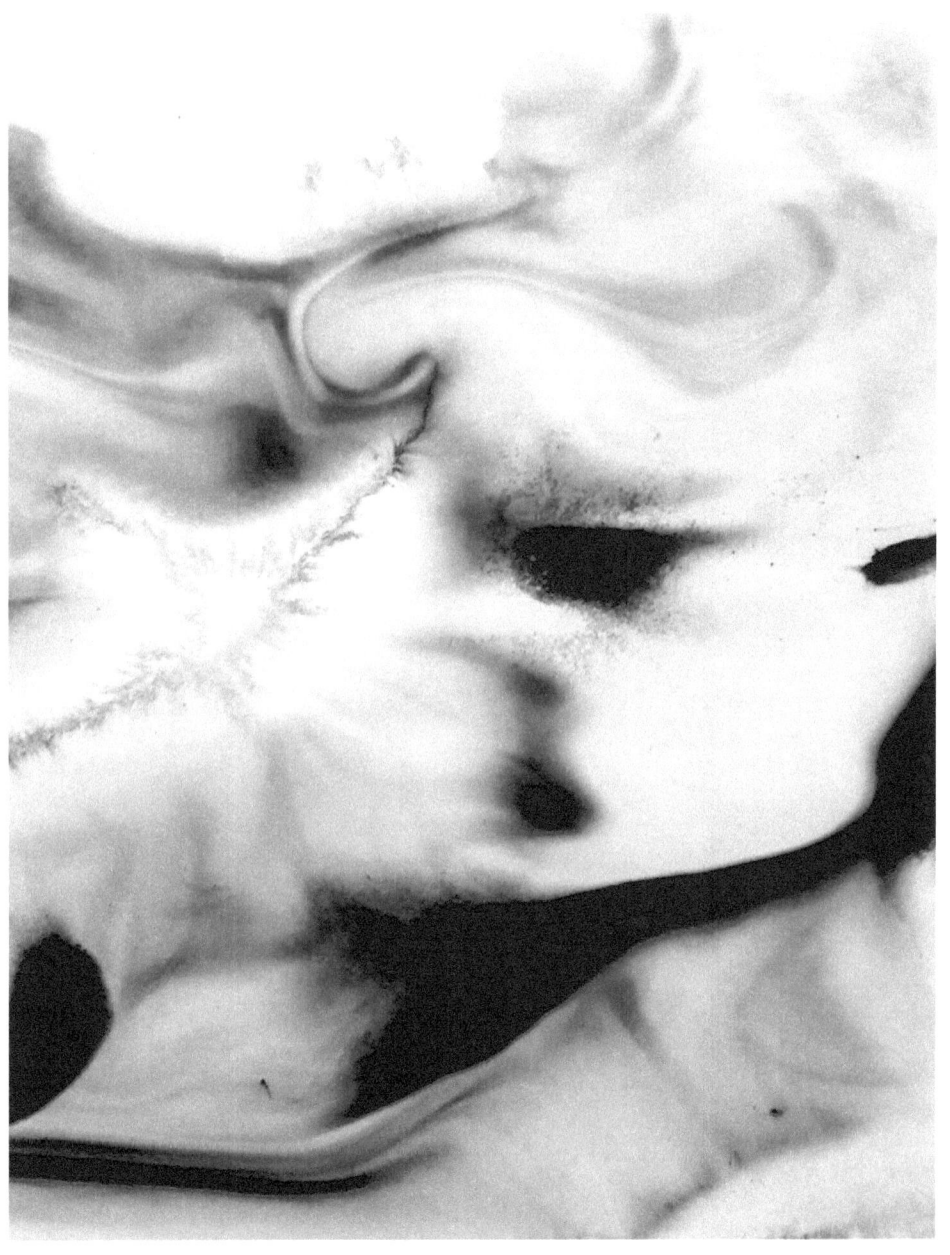

a chance to conceive the moon I'm tethered to

open lotus
a pond makes room
for the rain

daring to float her fertility

taking on water
the moon
fast approaching full

open carry
she begins
to show

between waxing and waning   first contraction

postpartum
a hole in the light
the shape of me

NO MORE WORDS

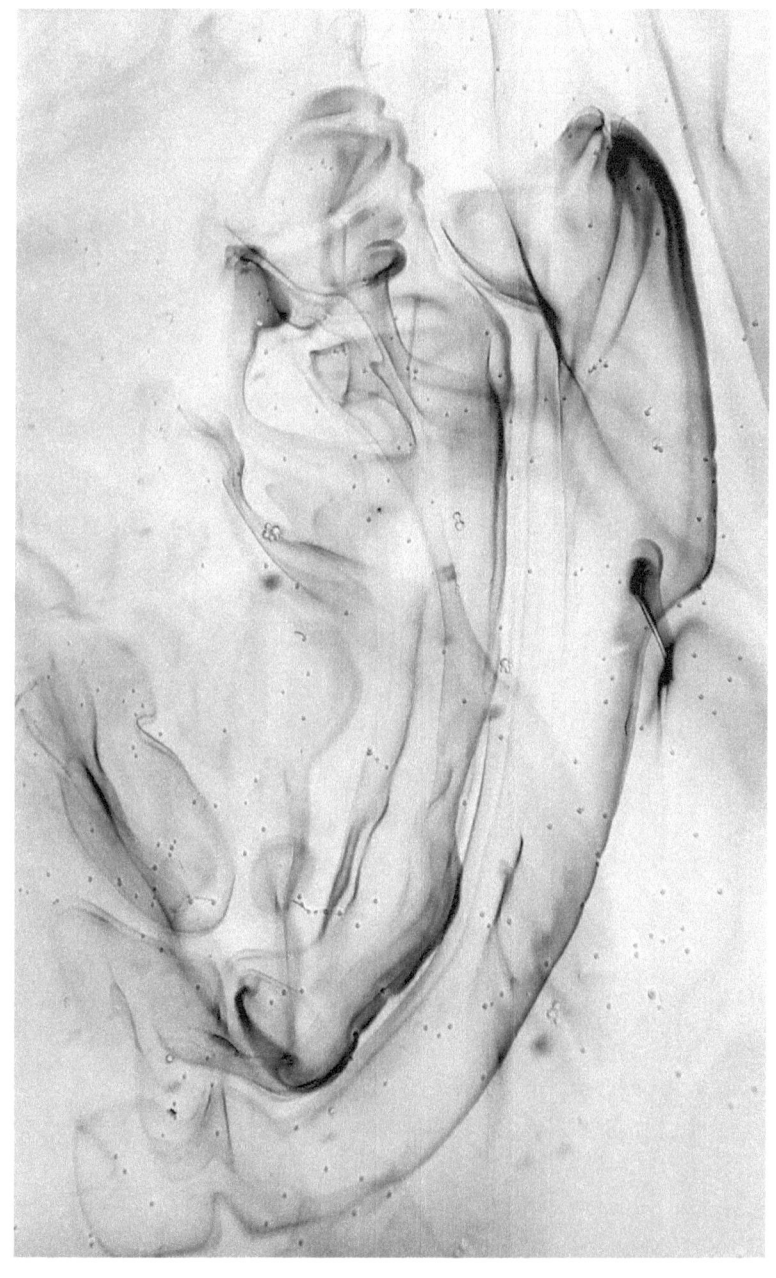

female cardinal
my closet
of earth tones

mirroring her pain-body goes up a size

in blue ink her inner burns silently surface

outgoing tide
footprints
that no longer fit

no more words
only clouds of frozen breath
between us

skin hunger
the caress
of her tears

this vow …
the paper leaves
of a winter beech

MIGRATING MONARCHS

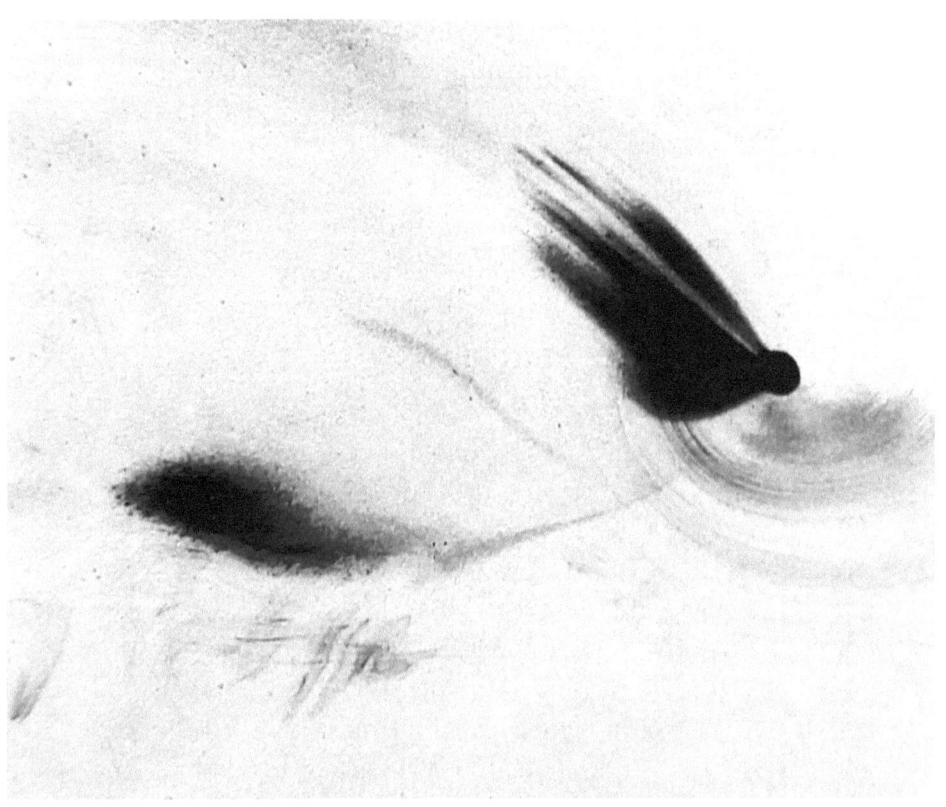

shelter window
such a thin pane
between us

their living wages war on lies of scarcity

pull of quicksand
her second-hand boots
missing their straps

the unhoused migrating monarchs with their cake

evacuation
the ones without
wings

all my irons in the fire out

already the month's end of the world again

COUNTING BLOSSOMS

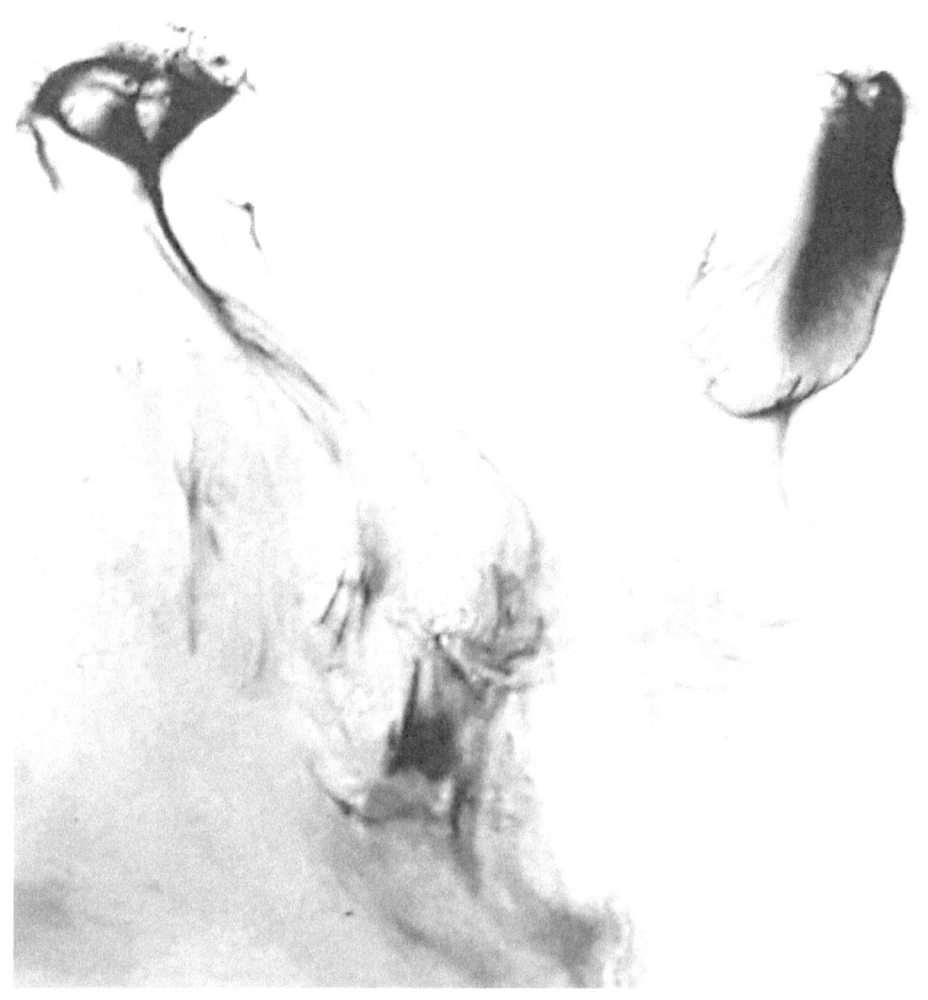

tea for one …
the prolonged scream
of the kettle

the care she takes in cutting her paper heart

young sea glass—
the numbness deeper
than last time

waning moon
trying so hard
to be full

addiction takes another holiday

support group …
the comfort of the chair
between us

counting blossoms
into her daughter's hands
one day at a time

A CARESS OF MOON

stepping off
the eggshell path
second spring

just me without a prefix

left behind
in the move
the bowl
all the other bowls
fit inside

unshelled cicada
a caress of moon
on new skin

early spring
the garden and I
work on each other

female rain …
an awakening of color
in the pebbled lane

her troubled past …
jars of sea glass
on the windowsill

WHISPERED RESISTANCE

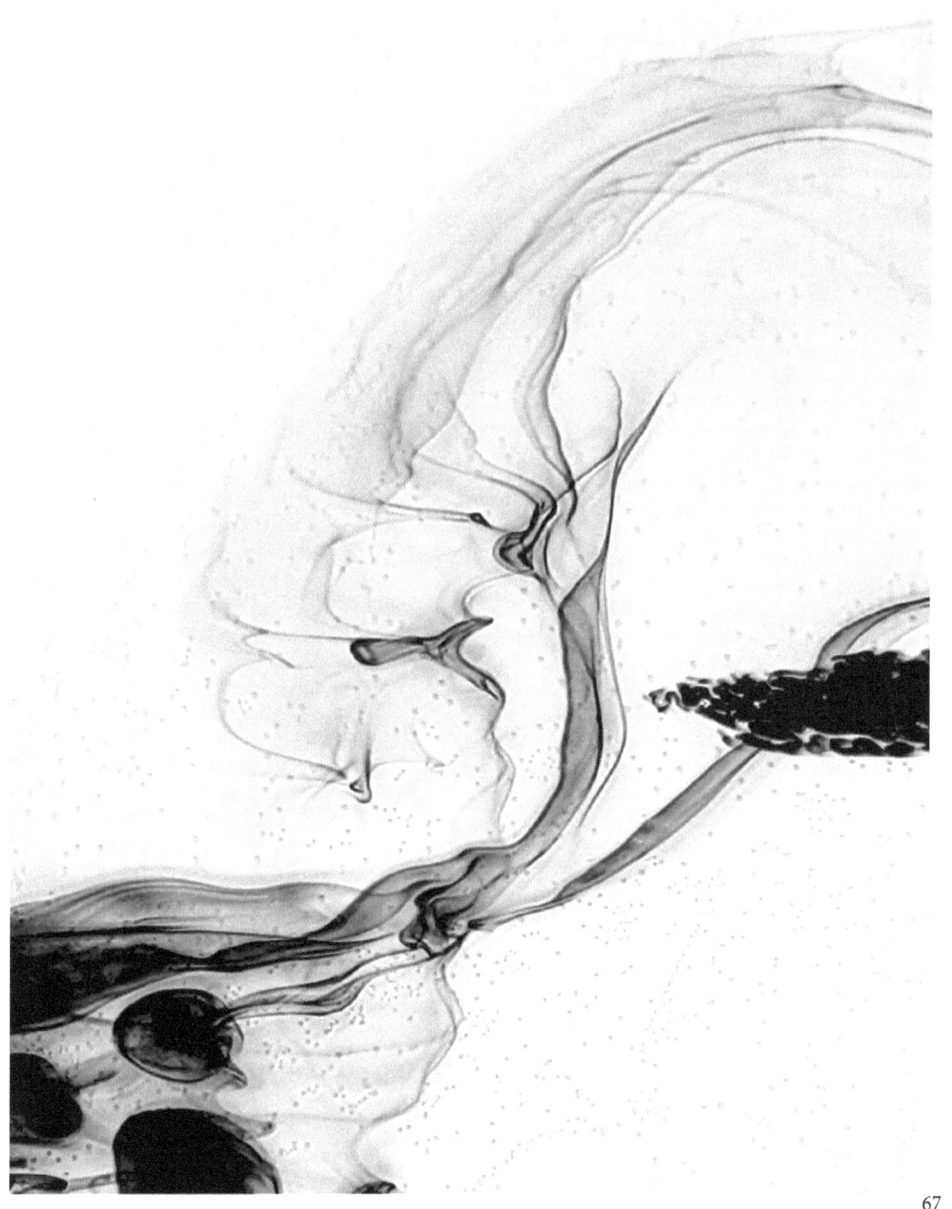

sun-soaked chrysalis
the effort
no one sees

freshwater pearls
trying on
another perspective

mourning cloaks a coming out celebration

preferred pronoun
today, an ice cube
for the orchid

rigidity the whispered resistance of prairie grass

daybreak in a chord each bird's given song

barefoot to make much of time in clover

WINTER FORSYTHIA

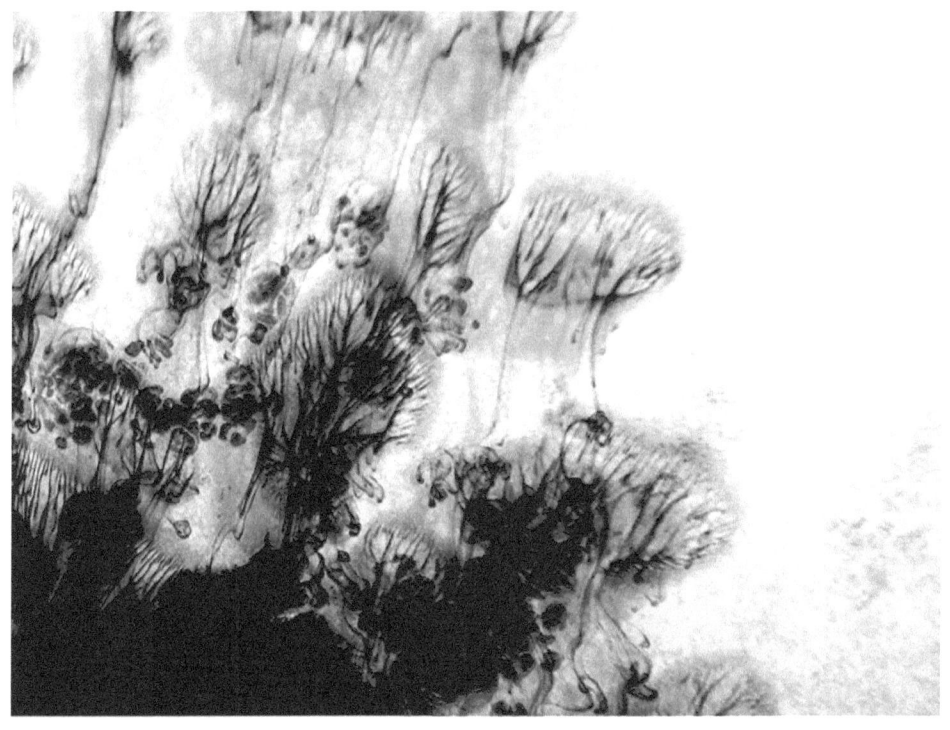

mid journey umbilical tugs fore and aft

empty nest
a dried tea bag
on her saucer

menopausal assumptions of winter forsythia

100,000 miles stuck in reverse puberty

cry for not my usual self help

molting season
so many lives
in this one

after changing my default settings

CATARACT CLOUDS

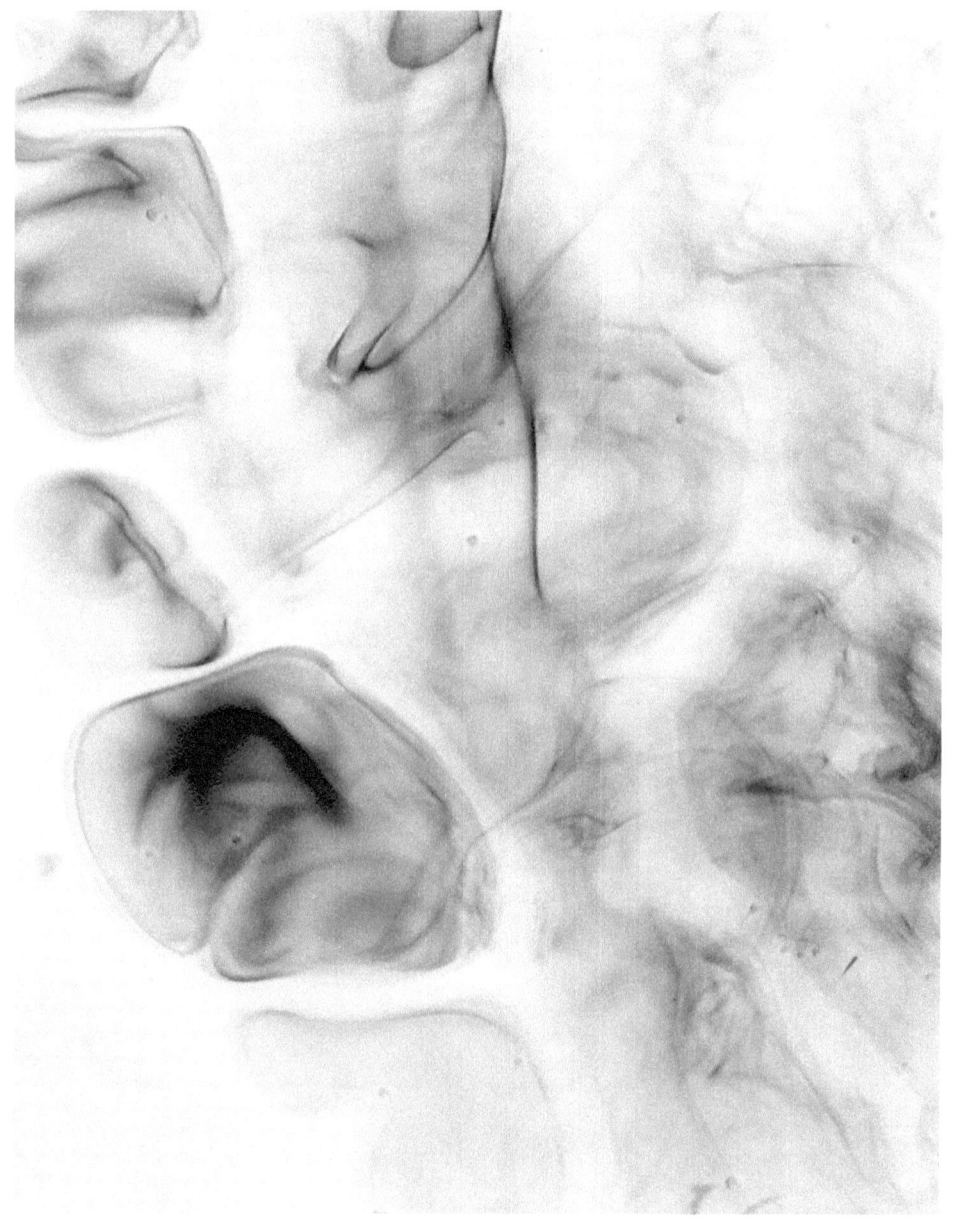

all the king's horses accepting my new normal

still the same winter pond still

memories leaving no tracks through the snow

breaching whale
the time between
too soon and too late

cataract clouds …
her children remind her
what she likes

glacial decay
i save another
sidewalk worm

all of us
witnesses
blood moon

fin

www.ingramcontent.com/pod-product-compliance
Lightning Source LLC
Chambersburg PA
CBHW030054170426
43197CB00010B/1522